Lean Business

By Ade Asefeso MCIPS MBA

Copyright 2014 by Ade Asefeso MCIPS MBA
All rights reserved.

First Edition

ISBN-13: 978-1502945242

ISBN-10: 150294524X

Publisher: AA Global Sourcing Ltd
Website: http://www.aaglobalsourcing.com

Table of Contents

Disclaimer 5
Dedication 6
Chapter 1: Introduction 7
Chapter 2: Rethinking the Lean Principles 11
Chapter 3: Lean Systemic Approach 15
Chapter 4: Why Lean Startup Changes Everything 39
Chapter 5: Lean Startup Strategy 45
Chapter 6: Starting On Little or No Funding 51
Chapter 7: Executing Lean Growth Strategies 55
Chapter 8: How to Build a Lean and Efficient Business Plan 59
Chapter 9: Questions to Ask Before Determining Your Target Market 63
Chapter 10: Skills People Need to Create a Lean Business 67
Chapter 11: Skills of a Lean Leader 83
Chapter 12: Goals of the CEO in a Lean Organization 87
Chapter 13: Lean Strategies for Business Process Improvement 89
Chapter 14: Lean Culture Require Enabling Structures 95
Chapter 15: A Lean Business is Customer Centric 103

Chapter 16: Profits from the Lean Business Model 105
Chapter 17: Becoming Lean Business with Analytics 109
Chapter 18: Conclusion 113

Disclaimer

This publication is designed to provide competent and reliable information regarding the subject matter covered. However, it is sold with the understanding that the author and publisher are not engaged in rendering professional advice. The authors and publishers specifically disclaim any liability that is incurred from the use or application of contents of this book.

If you purchased this book without a cover you should be aware that this book may have been stolen property and reported as "unsold and destroyed" to the publisher. In this case neither the author nor the publisher has received any payment for this "stripped book."

Dedication

To my family and friends who seems to have been sent here to teach me something about who I am supposed to be. They have nurtured me, challenged me, and even opposed me.... But at every juncture has taught me!

This book is dedicated to my lovely boys, Thomas, Michael and Karl. Teaching them to manage their finance will give them the lives they deserve. They have taught me more about life, presence, and energy management than anything I have done in my life.

Chapter 1: Introduction

A lean organisation understands customer value and focuses its key processes to continuously increase it. The ultimate goal is to provide perfect value to the customer through a perfect value creation process that has zero waste.

To accomplish this, lean thinking changes the focus of management from optimising separate technologies, assets, and vertical departments to optimising the flow of products and services through entire value streams that flow horizontally across technologies, assets, and departments to customers.

Eliminating waste along the entire value streams, instead of at isolated points, creates processes that need less human effort, less space, less capital, and less time to make products and services at far less costs and with much fewer defects, compared with traditional business systems. Companies are able to respond to changing customer desires with high variety, high quality, low cost, and with very fast throughput times; information management also becomes much simpler and more accurate.

The first approach to lean is the set of 'tools' that assist in the identification and steady elimination of waste (muda). As waste is eliminated, quality improves while production time and cost are reduced. These tools include:
1. Value Stream Mapping
2. 5S

3. Kanban (pull systems)
4. Total Productive Maintenance
5. Kaizan

The second approach to lean, is where the focus is upon improving the 'flow' or smoothness of work, thereby steadily eliminating mura ('unevenness') through the system and not just upon 'waste reduction'. Techniques to improve flow include production levelling, and 'pull' production (by means of Kanban).

The difference between these two approaches is not the goal itself, but rather the prime approach to achieving it. The implementation of smooth flow exposes quality problems that already existed, and thus waste reduction naturally happens as a consequence. The advantage for this approach is that it naturally takes a system-wide perspective, whereas a waste focus sometimes wrongly assumes this perspective.

Lean implementation is focused on getting the right things to the right place at the right time in the right quantity to achieve perfect work flow, while minimising waste and being flexible and able to change.

A popular misconception is that lean is suited only for manufacturing. Not true. Lean applies in every business and every process. It is not a tactic or a cost reduction program, but a way of thinking and acting for an entire organisation. Businesses in all industries and services; including healthcare and governments are using lean principles as the way they think and do.

Lean business principles lead to processes that minimize waste in delivering products or services to end users.

From the standpoint of lean thinking, value begins and ends with the customer. Customers require a particular product or service from your business, and you must provide it in the amount necessary and on the customer's schedule. Determining the product or service that provides value to the customer stands as the first task for the business.

Value Stream Mapping

Once you determine what provides value to the customer, you must figure out or map the processes and procedures that get that product or service to the customer. This mapping process calls for identifying the unnecessary steps that add no value or contribute to waste. For example, if you discover that employees must go through a complicated process to place orders into the computer system, you would likely flag that process as a waste contributor.

Flow

Creating flow refers to the formal removal of unnecessary steps that hinder delivery of a product or service to the customer. For example, if a cleaning service must routinely visit an off-site storage facility for supplies, this activity delays delivery of service. To enhance flow, the business might remodel to increase on-site storage space.

Pull

Pull calls for production on an as-needed basis; in essence, you produce in response to demand. In a service business where delivery depends on manpower, pull could translate into hiring on the basis of existing demand, rather than hiring on the basis on expected demand.

Perfection

Perfection calls for an ongoing refinement of the other four principles in a bid to achieve a zero-waste delivery process of service or product delivery. The guiding idea is that additional waste gets exposed over time. The refinement process also helps a business adapt to inevitable shifts in customer demands.

Considerations

The classic five principles of lean thinking may prove insufficient for the contemporary business situation. Businesses frequently apply lean thinking only to issues such as order fulfilment, with insufficient regard given to quality management, communication and leadership.

We proposes an eight-principle model of lean thinking that in theory, should address these issues and provide a less manufacturing-centric approach later in this book.

Chapter 2: Rethinking the Lean Principles

Since Lean Thinking was published in 1996, our understanding of what Lean is has moved on. Lean has now been applied across a wider range of manufacturing and service industries and the issue of sustaining change has become more central to the lean debate. As a result I believe it is now time to revisit the Womack and Jones five principles. In order to do this, it will be helpful to understand what the main areas of concerns might be.
1. Many organisations have failed to interpret the original principles well.
2. In hindsight, there are gaps or weaknesses in the original set.
3. The world has moved on.
4. Our understanding of how Lean works has improved.

These areas of concern lead to a number of specific problems. The first problem revolves around how Lean works in different industries and the fact that classic Lean texts tend, explicitly or implicitly, to assume that we all work in high volume, repetitive manufacturing environments such as car components or electronics industries.

There appears to be little allowance for people in low volume or more variable manufacturing industries or the service sector. What we have observed is that the further you take Lean from its car making origins, the more strained some of the classic principles become. For instance, in high variety manufacturing or service industries many struggle with the concept of kanban style pull systems. As a result, organisations such as a local private Hospital in the UK have redefined their own principles including; Focus on the Patient, Understand our Processes, Social and Technical Flows, Responsive Teams and Learn and Spread.

The next set of problems revolves around the fact that the original principles have been generally interpreted at an operational level. Many firms use Lean as a focus for point - kaizen improvement activities on the shop floor. Indeed, almost all the organisations we meet tend to look at physical flows only in the Order Fulfilment process (customer order to delivery of product or service).

As a result Lean is often used as a short term cost cutting or waste reduction mechanism. Indeed, many refer to Lean as a cost reduction toolkit, an initiative or a programme. Even Womack and Jones open their book with: "Muda. It's the one word of Japanese you really must know...muda means "waste"". In contrast if you seek out the Toyota corporate website you will find that Taiichi Ohno has a different perspective. "Eliminate muda, mura, muri....completely" What appears to be missing in the Lean Thinking book is the focus on levelling and making life easy for people.

Linked to this waste reduction focus, is another significant gap, the lack of an appropriate focus on quality and risk. Fundamental to the creation of a complete Lean Business System is achieving what the customer wants, when they want it. This implies the pursuit of 100% quality as well as 100% on time delivery. It also implies that risk is at an absolute minimum.

Rarely do we see Lean applied within the context of the business needs, wider environmental or social concerns, strategy formation or deployment. It is usually a tactical activity run by full, or part time, improvement agents. This lack of senior management involvement means that there is rarely appropriate senior level leadership and, as a result, insufficient attention to employee engagement. The result of this is that the sustainability of change is poor.

The reason for this is that the classic Lean Principles almost totally missed the importance of people. Specifically, little attention was drawn to the importance of communication supportive human resource policies, staff training and development.

In addition, inadequate attention was paid to the importance of resourcing the change process and individual job design. It is interesting to contrast that with some key reasons why Lean transitions fail. Finally, the classic Lean principles appear (or have been interpreted as being) too focused inside the organisation. As a result, few organisations outside of the automotive sector appear to take their Lean activities into their supply chain. The result is again often point-kaizen activity where single firms are the focus of improvement rather than the complete supply chain.

To summarise; the traditional Lean approach is too piecemeal, too short term in nature and with little focus on the areas required to make it sustainable in most organisations. What is called for is a more systemic approach.

Chapter 3: Lean Systemic Approach

Taking all the concerns in the last two chapters into account; we have redefined the original principles into a new Lean system approach; the 8Ps of the Lean Business System.

This framework helps companies in any industry, and at any stage of Lean maturity, to reflect on how they are deploying Lean in their business. It helps to take the focus away from point-kaizen activity towards a more contingent approach, a more aligned approach, a more human approach and ultimately, a more sustainable approach. Indeed it is part of a move to Lean becoming a cultural journey towards everyone in the organisation actively working towards a fully aligned 'tomorrow better than today' system.

We believe that this new 8Ps approach will also, at least to some degree, overcome the shortcoming of the classic Womack & Jones approach.

1. Purpose

Before starting any activity it is important to understand the purpose and to align the organisation.

Ask yourself, how many people in the organisations:
   a. Really understand what they are supposed to achieve?
   b. Feel they have an appropriate set of KPIs?

    c. Are working on too many things at once?
    d. Can point to how they are making tomorrow better than today?

So what do you need to take into account in developing a purpose?

Traditional management has taught us to focus on the Voice of the Owner. Traditional Lean Thinking has extending that to include the Voice of the Customer (although we rarely find that this is the starting point for a Lean transformation). Even this dual focus is not enough.

Focus on the Voice of the Owner and Voice of the Customer fails to focus on the muri; the frustrations and problems that individual people face in their work. It fails therefore to address the "what is in it for me?" objection to change. It fails to focus adequately on the Voice of the Employee. This concern is key and we will return to it in the section on People later in this chapter.

As our collective thinking has moved on, we now need to focus also on the Voice of Society. Specifically our role as corporate citizens and in particular the environmental impacts of our activities. We will again return to this area in the Planet section later in this chapter.

Codifying the purpose is a key job of the senior management team. It is a way of capturing the WHAT, the direction, the focus and ideas about the destination. If done well it is also a powerful tool in establishing the WHY. Focusing on these two areas is not only essential, but it will help senior managers start moving away from simply HOW based thinking. In my experience, pre-defined solutions from senior managers, often without much thinking about WHAT and WHY, often have only a poor chance of being accepted by the business and an even poorer chance of leading to sustainable change.

Not only do organisations need to have a purpose, they also need to communicate it in a way that engages the workforce. This almost certainly needs to be done in a visual way translating the purpose into a language that is accessible to people at their level of the organisation. It needs to be more than mere visual displays used to impress visitors, but a living, breathing management tool that is the focus of how the organisation is run.

2. Process

Having work with Lean for over 20 years; I find that the majority of firms still only apply Lean in one process; Order Fulfilment. Order Fulfilment starts with the customer's need, is translated into an information flow in the organisation and results in a reverse flow to the customer of the end product or service. This is the process that almost all organisations address in their Lean journey, either in whole or in part; 95% never get any further. In addition these 95% tend to be addressing cost reduction having done some Value Stream Mapping.

So why is this a problem? Mainly because they are only scratching the surface of what is possible with a Lean Business System. Businesses have many processes that they need to manage, and manage well; including ones that stretch across internal departments. In general there are three types.
a. Directional Processes.
b. Core Processes.
c. Enabling Processes

There is usually only one Directional Process in a business, often called strategic management and it is often only in this process and at this level that a cross-functional approach is taken. There are usually 3-6 Core Processes that deliver the main tangible outputs and outcomes for the business. These might include Innovation, Order Creation and Order Fulfilment. In addition to these there are 3-6 Enabling Processes that support the Core Processes to deliver the key business result.

Each process has its own part to play, but it is the Core Processes that are likely to deliver on the majority of the top level strategy and KPI set; however, across different organisations, this may be in radically different ways.

Improvements in the Order Fulfilment process are likely to deliver an increase in capacity in order to achieve a cost benefit. Many businesses go wrong here, however, because they assume that is the goal of Lean. In many cases there is a dislocation between the business strategy and this 'Lean' cost reduction. Worse than this, many of the cost savings are often illusory. What for instance is the cost saving of merely freeing up 20% of a factory or office block on its own? There may be some, but it usually far from 20% of the total costs.

If we instead think of Lean more holistically, as an approach to deliver improved customer service and waste reduction, then the outcome should be an increase in profitable growth. In other words lean should deliver an optimal balance between these two areas aligned to the business goals and purpose; however, how can organisations do this if they are usually only addressing one single process whose improvement is likely to be largely about reducing cost? The answer is, of course, that they can't, not unless they seek to improve a range of other processes such as Order Creation and Innovation.

The improvement of these processes is less likely to be about reducing cost and more about improving customer value. In other words they are about growing the business or filling capacity.

We call this X and 2X thinking as this links to the profit potential of Lean in an organisation. By creating capacity through the improvement of processes like Order Fulfilment a business may achieve some cost reduction and hence deliver on some profit potential it may have had; however, it is only when this capacity is utilised when processes such as Innovation and Order Creation are addressed that the full benefit will be reaped by the business. In my experience the profit potential benefit of filling this capacity is never less than twice as large as the benefit in creating the capacity. In some cases the ratio can be as much as X to 10X.

3. People

The area of people is misunderstood by many organisations applying Lean. One of my reflections on re-reading Womack & Jones's Lean Thinking is that the key issue in the success of the case study firms was not the tools, shop floor improvements or kaikaku events (Large-scale, radical change). It was in the leadership of the senior executives. This reflection has been borne out many times in the times that I and my colleagues have witnessed effective and sustainable change.

Linked to leadership is the ability to engage people in the business. Toyota talks about Respect for People. This means allowing the people who know the job best; the people who do the work to work out HOW we are going to improve. Developing a culture of Continuous Improvement is not sufficient without this fundamental respect for people.

The People principle is without doubt fundamental to the success and sustainability of any Lean transformation. We will highlight 8 areas that need to be addressed.

a. Understanding the difference between management and leadership

In general much of our career progression, HR policies and education system are designed to create high quality managers. This is essential to deliver today's results and keep organisations working; however, it is insufficient to create an effective tomorrow. To innovate, develop, inspire or challenge existing businesses. We need to manage and lead.

This dual role has most effectively been translated by Honda who uses the concept of Futatsue Shigoto or 'two jobs'. By this they talk about Today's Job (managing what I need to do now to be successful) and Tomorrow's Job (leading in terms of what I need to do to be successful in the future). Honda emphasises that each one of them is equally important.

b. Creating and deploying an inspiring vision

Part of the leadership role is to inspire people to want to change. It is about creating a vision, a direction, something for everyone to be inspired by. This can either be the avoidance of something bad, the 'burning platform', or better still a destination people want to achieve.

c. Defining, demonstrating and encouraging correct behaviours

The third area is about creating a culture where an appropriate behaviour set is instilled right across the business. The starting point is to establish which behaviours are appropriate, ensure they are 'lived' and demonstrated by the senior team and then find mechanisms to do this across the workforce.

These involve:
    i.   Customer consciousness.

ii. Enterprise thinking.
  iii. Adaptation.
  iv. Taking initiative.
  v. Innovation.
  vi. Collaboration.
  vii. Influence

  d. Aligning support policies and procedures with purpose

When trying to implement a Lean approach it is necessary to ensure that the various supporting structures are aligned to the purpose. We have already talked about the right KPIs and their deployment. Equally important is the alignment of HR and accounting policies and procedures. This is necessary as these policies and procedures underpin the required workforce characteristics which in themselves underpin the commercial and cultural outcomes of a lean programme.

The most important of these HR policies and procedures is how people's performance is managed, their reward and recognition defined, their training and development undertaken and their succession planning run. We will return to the training and development area in the Pull section later in this chapter.

To illustrate the other areas, let's follow the 7 Lean Skills. These were applied to the annual performance review by a company I use to work for. Each manager had one to one discussions with employee about how they had exhibited these skills. Decisions on reward, recognition and promotion were equally weighted. As a result people were promoted who had the right attitudes, not just fire-fighting skills.

e. Creating a dynamic communication system

In my experience the best performing organisations have the best communications systems, using a variety of methods to mirror different preferences that people have for absorbing information and providing feedback. What is important is that the communications are simple, well thought through, in a language and medium that are likely to be understood and are two-way.

I have often found that the use of visual cues with appropriate data works well. As a good friend of mine once said to me when reflecting on the reasons for their success, "It was all about three things; communication, communication and communication".

f. Developing Situational Leadership

Another important area within the People principle is adopting the appropriate leadership style at each stage of a Lean transformation. A business goes through a journey when applying Lean. This usually starts with a rather ad hoc or reactive management system and progresses over time to an autonomous 'way of life' style where there is no longer a need to give the work a title such as Lean or Continuous Improvement.

At each stage of the journey a different leadership style is required. Near the beginning a championing or driving approach is required. This involves senior managers and lean coaches getting things going, making projects work and getting early results.

Later on the journey a more supportive or mentoring style is required to support the line in their lean journey. We will return to this change in style in the Pull section later in this chapter.

g. Working on Job Design

In order to move the focus away from just doing the day job to thinking about creating a better tomorrow, it is also necessary to consider job design at all levels of the organisation. Consider the typical split of working time for executives, middle managers and operatives.

What you typically find is that executives spend some time working on strategy, although frequently too much on big bang top-down HOW-focused programmes that are then handed to middle managers to implement. This means they need to engage operatives; however, the operatives' line managers are often reluctant to free them up as they do not want to see time wasted on what they perceive to be 'non productive' activity.

The result of this is that the day job predominates at these levels; however, it also means that any change that is undertaken is likely to be quick-hit with only a low chance of being sustained. As a consequence fundamental problems and weaknesses don't get properly addressed and much of the executive and middle manager time gets taken up in fire-fighting. Does this sound familiar?

In contrast, we could envisage an ideal state where everyone in the business spends some time working on strategy. This is not to say that everyone will work on high level strategy, but more on strategy as it affects them. In other words, within their environment, how can they make tomorrow better than today to achieve their part of the purpose? To make these improvements they will also need a formal time budget to achieve these gains. Even at operative levels these two elements may be as much as 15% of their working time; however, only by making this investment, will the day job be improved and a continuous improvement mentality established.

Clearly here we are looking at an ideal state that might take many years to achieve. Hence each business will need to define its own future states over successive Lean roadmaps towards this ideal state.

h. Leading by not leading

The last area is leading by not leading, a paradox for the senior team. This relates to the activities of the executives within the improvement segment. Let's say that a business invests 10% of the formal time of all its employees on improvement. Within this, the senior team should minimise the amount of time they spend on big-bang top down (often disengaging) initiatives and maximise the amount of time they invest in small, local bottom up projects.

An example may be a plant or office manager spending 2-3 days a month taking part in local projects. The trick is not to lead the projects, nor facilitate them, nor manage them. It is to just be a team member asking permission of the team to just take part and offer outside-the-box suggestions, as they are the least likely person in the team to understand the work in detail. This 'not leading' approach however shows a great deal of leadership and is likely to inspire many across the business to want to improve as they see just how seriously Lean is being taken by the executive team. This may sound strange, but if applied well, certainly works.

4. Pull

There are three main areas of pull that are necessary to consider within a Lean Business System. These will be discussed in turn.

i. Pull-Based Delivery

Within the traditional Lean approach airtime is rightly given to the creation of flow and pull. One of the problems here is that much of the Lean books tends to be written by, or for, people working in a high volume manufacturing environment where demand variability is low. Example of this might include the car or electronics industry. People who do not work in these environments can find the concept of pull difficult to interpret and apply, a prime example being the office environment.

Hence, it is my belief that although pull-based delivery is desirable, in many cases it is hard, if not impossible to achieve. In addition, in a transition to a full Lean approach, it may not be the first and most important focus for activity. I have seen too many manufacturing firms attempting to create a pull system in an unstable process environment leading to disaster. We will return to this area in the Prevention section later in this chapter.

So why might pull be hard or impossible to achieve? In some industries the quantity of product or service is very high and the variability of demand very low. Typical of this might be industries producing components or products for mass markets such as bread, toothpaste or milk. We call such cases Runner products.

In other extreme cases we might find that volumes are very low and orders highly variable. Industries producing parts for classic cars or the space industry may be regarded as producing stranger products.

In between these extremes a range of products or services with intermediary levels of demand and variability may be regarded as Repeater products. The majority of Lean books assumes we all live and work in a 'runner' world where well-constructed kanban based pull systems can operate. Clearly this is not true.

Ideally the first job in a Lean environment is to understand the customer and their pull-based demands. Before even doing this it might be useful to differentiate between real demand and created demand. Consider, for instance buying a car. On entering the dealer you see the car you want but the showroom model is red instead of blue. You enquire about getting a blue one and are quoted a 6 week lead time. As an alternative you are offered the red car with a 10% discount. You decide to buy the red car. Is this real demand or created demand?

In most companies this would be treated as real demand and hence under a kanban system, particularly if replicated many times, could lead to major distortions of supply. In fact, we would be dealing with a distorted demand rather than the true Voice of the Customer. So the first step might be differentiating between real demand and the created demand resulting from a failure of the system.

The second task might then be to try to find ways to reduce the variability of demand (for instance by reducing the lead-time) or increasing the effective volume of demand (for instance by standardising or modularising different offerings).

The third task would then be to establish the appropriate type of supply system for the resulting product or service. Here a kanban-based pull system might be most appropriate for a runner and a make-to-order flow system for a repeater; however, in the rare occasions where it is not possible to move the product or service out of the stranger zone it may still be necessary to operate under push based conditions.

ii. Pull-Based Improvement

In most of the organisations I visit; it's difficult to find a link between the improvement activity that is going on and the needs of the business, the customers, the employees or wider society. In many cases what is improved seem to be more a whim of a particular, usually senior level, person. Indeed, when I look in detail at the programme of improvement set out by many firms I can see little or no link to their professed strategy. The question is, are we solving the right problems? If not, it seems almost inevitable that even a well delivered improvement programme will be ultimately considered to be a failure.

I also observe in many organisations that projects or programmes are conceived by senior management and, as we saw within the People principle area, are then imposed on local people by full time change agents. If this situation is particularly severe or continues for a protracted time I hear complaints from people lower down in the organisational structure that they have been 'Leaned'. This push based mentality rarely has little to do with the needs of the business, customer, (local) employees or society. It is more often driven by flawed metrics such the need for so many kaizen events or black belt projects in a given time period. This piecemeal approach is likely to lead to disengagement, frustration and poor sustainability. Unfortunately I find these symptoms far too often within organisations employing push-based improvement.

To create an effective Lean Business System, it is necessary to move as quickly as possible to a pull-based improvement system. This does not necessarily mean immediately, as the speed and priority of moving quickly to a pull-based approach will vary depending on the business situation, the Lean maturity of the business and the competing needs for rapid development of other areas of the Lean Business System; however, in general, I would say the transition should at least start within the first two years of any transformation.

So what are the key ingredients of a pull-based improvement system?

First, there needs to be absolute clarity on what the business is trying to achieve (including a focus on the customer, employees and society). Second, this WHAT needs to be communicated in a highly effective way so that everyone in the organisation can understand what the business is trying to achieve, what this means to them and their team (including their contribution to it) and an effective, aligned and engaging set of KPIs. Third, and perhaps most crucial, is that the problems being solved and projects to be worked on have been selected by the team at that level. In other words that the ownership resides locally pulled by the local needs for improvement rather than pushed by a senior management group who might be quite remote from the workplace.

iii. Pull-Based Training

Closely linked to pull-based improvement is the concept of pull-based training. This contrasts with the classic push-based training seen far too frequently in business. Within push-based training the topics, duration and timing of courses are pushed by the needs of some senior management group, typically the training manager.

In contrast, within a pull-based approach, training is undertaken according to the needs of the local team and is decided by consultation of the team leader (at whichever) level and the individual. It is based on a skills and competency needs that the team have in order to make their contribution to the success of the business.

It is hence impossible to have pulled-based training unless pull-based improvement is in place. The first time I observed this element of the Lean Business System was when working with the Toyota supply chain. When I benchmarked their performance against a similar supply chain the UK; I found that the gaps were enormous. One surprise was the fact that the employees in the Japanese firms spent on average only half the amount of hours doing training but clearly hugely outperformed their western counterparts in terms of results.

The reason for this was two-fold. First, the Toyota suppliers in Japan were operating a pull-based training approach and second 90% of their training was On-The-Job (or as they called it OJT) rather than less than the 10% more typical in the west.

5. Prevention

One of the most serious errors I see in the use of Lean is an excessive focus on tools and techniques. Not only this, but in many cases this focus is highly skewed towards a few tools. Among the ones I most frequently encounter are.
a. Value Stream Mapping.

b. 5S
c. Kanban
d. Quick Changeovers (SMED)

These are all good tools; however, they are often applied in a slavish way. Worse still, little allowance is made to whether they are the right tools or other more appropriate tools are required. These tools are focused on preventing variation, problems and subsequent rework or quality failures for the customer.

The result is that organisations are trying to improve the flow of an unstable system. This is very unlikely to work. This failure within the traditional Lean approach (as applied by many) has led more enlightened organisations to try to fill the gap by collecting a series of tools to address the problem. The most prominent of these are the Six Sigma tools first collated by Motorola in the 1980s. Although this was a good reaction to the problem they saw in many limited lean organisations, their mistake was to then not employ the other tools that were being used. Hence, there became an imbalance with an over focus on the Quality pillar side of the true Lean Business System.

What is required is a balance of tools from the Tool House of Lean. This balance should be pulled by the needs for local improvement where there is a "daily habit" of continuous improvement that uses simple, visual technologies, tools and techniques that have been chosen and adapted for effective use. Hence, the specific tools to be used should be contingently selected according to specific needs.

6. Partnering

No company or organisation is an island and to create a world class organisation usually requires the creation of a world class supply chain. Indeed, the leading practitioners of Lean worldwide such as Toyota have also heavily focused on creating a high performing supply chain.

Indeed, when I compared the relative performance of Toyota's Japanese supply chain with a comparative one in the UK I found that the management of the supply chain was Toyota's key competitive advantage.

The question is, why? After six months of extensive research I discovered that the reason was that Toyota invested a huge amount of effort into partnering with their suppliers. In doing so they made dramatic improvements to their performance. Not only that, but Toyota had also taught their suppliers how to do the same using an approach they call Kyoryoku Kai or Supplier Association.

Unfortunately, although this inter-company development and coordination is at the heart of a true Lean Business System there are few companies in the West outside of the automotive industry that have got anywhere near achieving the type of results we see from Toyota. One of the main reasons is that insufficient focus has been given to the Partnering Principle in traditional Lean businesses.

7. Planet

It was just after the turn of the millennium that Jim Womack wrote: "Lean thinking must be "green" because it reduces the amount of energy and wasted by-products required to produce a given product. Indeed, examples are often cited of reducing human effort, space, and scrap by 50 percent or more, per product produced, through applying lean principles in an organisation; this means that lean's role is to be green's critical enabler as the massive waste in our current practices is reduce"; however, apart from a strong movement in the west coast of the United States, progress seems to have been slow on adopting the Planet as part of a wider set of Lean Business System Principles. This is in spite of the relentless march of Lean across industry sectors and the heightened awareness of the environment.

One of the first to put the green agenda on the map was the then Norwegian Prime Minister, Dr Gro Harlem Bruntland when she introduced the concept of sustainable development, describing it as being made up of three areas; economic, social and environmental sustainability.

For a company we might translate this as a focus on a 'respect for profit' (economic), 'respect for people' (social) and 'respect for environment' (environmental). To think in very simple terms.
    a. A traditional Lean approach might be described as understanding customer's needs and values and then reviewing the system and

processes that produces them so that the traditional eight wastes can be minimised.

b. Green might be described as understanding society's needs and values and then reviewing the system and processes that delivers them so that the eight environmental wastes can be minimised.

So what is the difference? Well apart from the fact that individual customers are multiplied to become society and the environmental wastes have a slightly different character than the traditional lean wastes, not a lot.

What is necessary is to include a set of diagnostic mapping tools and implementation tools that addresses the wider Planet issues and the Voice of Society.

8. Perfection

Perfection has been the 'holy grail' for Lean businesses since Womack and Jones encapsulated this principle in the mid 1990s. This focus was the result of a revision in thinking after a great deal of benchmarking work. The 1990s automotive research work showed us that there were huge gaps between the best and other companies. The gap, as we have seen it, was often between Toyota (or its supply chain) and western equivalents.

This benchmarking gave many western companies a wake-up call; however, it had two major problems in terms of energising organisations. First, partly because the gaps were so big, many organisations, particularly outside of the automotive sector, found it hard to accept the data. This led to reasons for inaction such as "they have a different culture, it is a different industry" and we are different".

Second, even those who were compelled by the data lacked a roadmap of how to move forward. As a result many organisations, often guided by external consultants, simply followed the quick fix kaizen blitz route leading in many cases to a poorly sustained short-term Lean initiative.

To counter this piecemeal approach, we believe that organisations should create their own Lean Business System. This requires them to develop a vision of their specific perfection and their own bespoke roadmap on how to move towards it. But how?

Simply put, the process is similar to best practice Value Stream Mapping, except here we are working at the business, rather than the Value Stream or process level. You then envision Perfection or the Ideal State (or what you think is the best possible position you could possibly reach). You then back off from this to a point that your team believe is feasible in the long term. This Feasible Future State might be 3 to 5 years away.

The next step is then to create a realistic point that can be reached within a sensible engaging timescale (usually around 18 months). This is the Targeted Future State that then requires a Roadmap. Once this

Targeted Future State position is achieved, a further Roadmap towards the Ideal State may then be created and deployed.

In this chapter we have sought to reflect on the state of Lean as it is today, through the lens of the traditional Lean Principles. These reflections have led me to conclude that some updating is necessary if organisations are to get further than the often tool based approach that I see.

We believe that the journey and the newly modified set of Principles we describe here are an essential part in creating for each organisation their own unique Lean Business System. Such a system can be used to create a holistic, integrated and engaging journey that will lead to sustainable long-term success.

Chapter 4: Why Lean Startup Changes Everything

Launching a new business; whether it's a tech startup, a small business, or an initiative within a large corporation; has always been a hit-or-miss proposition. According to the decades-old formula, you write a business plan, pitch it to investors, assemble a team, introduce a product, and start selling as hard as you can. Somewhere in this sequence of events, you will probably suffer a fatal setback. The odds are not with you. As new research shows, 75% of all startups fail.

But recently an important countervailing force has emerged, one that can make the process of starting a company less risky. It's a methodology called the "lean startup," and it favours experimentation over elaborate planning, customer feedback over intuition, and iterative design over traditional "big design up front" development. Although the methodology is just a few years old, its concepts such as "minimum viable product" and "pivoting" have quickly taken root in the startup world, and business schools have already begun adapting their curricula to teach them.

The lean startup movement hasn't gone totally mainstream, however we have yet to feel its full impact. In many ways it is roughly where the big data movement was five years ago; consisting mainly of a buzzword that is not yet widely understood, whose implications companies are just beginning to grasp.

But as its practices spread, they are turning the conventional wisdom about entrepreneurship on its head. New ventures of all kinds are attempting to improve their chances of success by following its principles of failing fast and continually learning. Despite the methodology's name, in the long term some of its biggest payoffs may be gained by the large companies that embrace it.

In this chapter I will offer a brief overview of lean startup techniques and how they have evolved. Most important, I will explain how, in combination with other business trends, they could ignite a new entrepreneurial economy.

The Fallacy of the Perfect Business Plan

According to conventional wisdom, the first thing every founder must do is create a business plan; a static document that describes the size of an opportunity, the problem to be solved, and the solution that the new venture will provide. Typically it includes a five-year forecast for income, profits, and cash flow. A business plan is essentially a research exercise written in isolation at a desk before an entrepreneur has even begun to build a product. The assumption is that it's possible to figure out most of the unknowns of a business in advance, before you raise money and actually execute the idea.

Once an entrepreneur with a convincing business plan obtains money from investors, he or she begins developing the product in a similarly insular fashion. Developers invest thousands of man-hours to get it ready for launch, with little if any customer input. Only after building and launching the product does the venture get substantial feedback from customers; when the sales force attempts to sell it and too often, after months or even years of development, entrepreneurs learn the hard way that customers do not need or want most of the product's features.

After decades of watching thousands of startups follow this standard routine, we have now learned at least three things:

1. Business plans rarely survive first contact with customers. As the boxer Mike Tyson once said about his opponents' prefight strategies. "Everybody has a plan until they get punched in the mouth."

2. No one besides venture capitalists and the late Soviet Union requires five-year plans to forecast a series of unknowns. These plans are generally fiction, and dreaming them up is almost always a waste of time.

3. Startups are not smaller versions of large companies. They do not unfold in accordance with master plans. The ones that ultimately succeed go quickly from failure to failure, all the while adapting, iterating on, and improving their initial ideas as they continually learn from customers.

Existing companies execute a business model, startups search for one. This distinction is at the heart of the lean startup approach. It shapes the lean definition of a startup; a temporary organization designed to search for a repeatable and scalable business model.

The Customer Development model breaks out all the customer-related activities of an early-stage company into four easy-to-understand steps. The first two steps of the process outline the "search" for the business model. Steps three and four "execute" the business model that is been developed, tested, and proven in steps one and two. The steps:

1. Customer discovery first captures the founders' vision and turns it into a series of business model hypotheses. Then it develops a plan to test customer reactions to those hypotheses and turn them into facts.

2. Customer validation tests whether the resulting business model is repeatable and scalable. If not, you return to customer discovery.

3. Customer creation is the start of execution. It builds end-user demand and drives it into the sales channel to scale the business.

4. Company-building transitions the organization from a startup to a company focused on executing a validated model.

In the "search" steps, you want a process designed to be dynamic, so you work with a rough business model description knowing it will change. The business model changes because startups use customer development to run experiments to test the hypotheses that make up the model. (First testing their understanding of the customer problem and then solutions.) Most of the time these experiments fail. Search embraces failure as a natural part of the startup process. Unlike existing companies that fire executives when they fail to match a plan, we keep the founders and change the model.

Once a company has found a business model (it knows its market, customers, product/service, channel, pricing, etc.), the organization moves from search to execution.

Searching for a business model requires a different organization from the one used to execute a plan. Searching requires the company to be organized around a customer development team led by the founders. It's only the founders who can make the strategic decisions to iterate and/or pivot the business model, and to do that they need to hear customer feedback directly. In contrast, execution (which follows search) assumes that the job specifications for each of the senior roles in the company can be tightly authored. Execution requires the company to be organized by function (product management, sales, marketing, business development, etc.)

Companies in execution suffer from a "fear of failure culture," quite understandable since they were hired to execute a known job specification. Startups with Customer Development Teams have a "learning and discovery" culture for search. The fear of making a move before the last detail is nailed down is one of the biggest problems existing companies have when they need to learn how to search.

The idea of not having a functional organization until the organization has found a proven business model is one of the hardest things for new startups to grasp. There are no sales, marketing or business development departments when you are searching for a business model. If you have organized your startup with those departments, you are not really doing customer development. It's like trying to implement a startup using Waterfall engineering.

Chapter 5: Lean Startup Strategy

Most startups fail because they waste too much time and money building the wrong product before realizing too late what the right product should have been.

Rather than spending months in stealth mode, a lean startup launches as quickly as possible with a "minimum viable product" (MVP), a bare-bones product that includes just enough features to allow useful feedback from early adopters. The company then continues hypothesis testing with a succession of incrementally refined product versions.

Lean startup executives do not invest in scaling the company until they have achieved product market fit (PMF); that is, the knowledge that they have developed a solution that matches the problem.

In lean startup lingo, "pivoting" refers to a major change in a company's direction based on user feedback. How entrepreneurs can stay true to their vision while still maintaining the flexibility to pivot.

Adhering to a lean startup strategy is especially challenging for companies that require a great deal of time to launch a workable product, such as clean-tech or biotech companies.

A dozen years ago, it seemed like all it took to launch a successful technology company was a vague idea, a PowerPoint presentation, a trade-show booth with a sexy spokes model and a URL. Then the dot.com bubble burst and investors got wiser and warier. Gone are the days when entrepreneurs could spend years burning through venture capital while they figured out their strategy. These are the days of the lean startup.

Most startups fail not because they can't build the product they set out to build, but because they build the wrong product, take too long to do that, waste a lot of money doing that, and waste a lot of money on sales and marketing trying to sell that wrong product. It takes a lot of time, time equals money, the money runs out, and the startup fails painfully.

Lean startups don't try to scale up the business until they have product market fit, a magical event-more easily recognized in retrospect than in the moment when they finally have a solution that matches the problem.

For starters, it nixes the traditional idea of a company spending several months in stealth mode while perfecting a full-featured product and planning an expensive launch party at a Las Vegas trade show. Rather, the lean startup launches as quickly as possible with what is call a minimum viable product (MVP), a product that includes just enough features to allow useful feedback from early adopters. This makes it easier for the company to speed to market with subsequent customer-driven versions of the product and it mitigates the likelihood of a company wasting time on features that nobody wants.

The MVP is a controversial idea because it can be perceived as something thrown together with shoestring and bubblegum but through a series of MVPs, a lean startup can validate a specific and comprehensive set of hypotheses about what the business is, where it's going, and what it has to do.

The Dropbox team initially announced a bare-bones version of its service on the website Hacker News. The company collected reams of immediate feedback from site readers, and continued to incorporate feedback into several successive product launches-each of which added only a couple of new features. While the feature additions were gradual, they were rapid, as was company growth. Dropbox increased its user base from 100,000 to 4 million in the course of 15 months.

Aardvark, which enables users to garner answers to questions via an extended network of friends' friends, used a Wizard-of-Oz-inspired method in its early days. Rather than building out the technology infrastructure to make their idea a reality, the team launched the service with humans routing users' questions "behind the curtain" instead of computers. This allowed the company to observe how and what users were asking and then spend time and money on a technology backbone that would best meet their needs.

Lean startups don't try to scale up the business until they have product market fit (PMF), a magical event more easily recognized in retrospect than in the moment when they finally have a solution that matches the problem and after you have that solution you can step on the gas pedal.

Of course, in carving a path to the PMF, startups may find that they have to shift the company in a completely new direction. In lean startup lingo, it's a process known as "pivoting."

Pivoting simply means making a major change of some sort. In lean startup logic, it's something you do, ideally, after you have run some decisive test to disprove a hypothesis. It can be changing the target customer segments by narrowing or broadening them. It can be changing the product itself, either by adding features or by taking features away. It can be a dramatic change. For example it could be we were going business-to-consumer, but we should be going business-to-business. Or it can be a change in business model. We were doing transaction-based pricing, but we have realized we should be doing subscription-based pricing. The notion of a pivot is to make a change, and ideally, after you pivot, you have a new set of assumptions and hypotheses that you are going to test.

There is a core problem inherent in pivoting; the risk of looking disloyal to the company vision. A startup's founders have worked so hard to sell employees, investors, customers, and partners on an idea that switching gears can feel almost like a betrayal; so much of what a CEO has to do is talk people into things. If you have to take people away from what you sold them on, that is hard.

We acknowledges that the lean startup methodology is easier to apply in the field of web-based startups than in the clean tech and biotech fields, both of which often require a great deal of time and capital to create any workable product. The same is true of the transportation industry. It is the nature of some products that you have to spend a whole lot of money before you know if the product is going to work.

Chapter 6: Starting On Little or No Funding

I really do think you can run your business on a shoestring budget and still get it to grow and be successful.

The phrase "lean startup" is a catch-all for any new business. But just how lean can you be when getting your new business on its feet?

I friend of mine a personal trainer at my local gym had no cash to get her business off the ground. The gym she worked at had just closed and she was determined to get another job as soon as she could.

So when a former client suggested she start a running club and offered herself up as the first customer, the fitness fanatic jumped at the opportunity.

"I really started with nothing, but soon realised that any money I was earning from paying clients needed to go straight back into the business," "I knew I had to spend some money on the business to grow it, but I also needed money to live on." she says.

The business she set-up then operates across United Kingdom. Her success proves a business can get starting on little, or no, funding.

"Now that my business has really grown, I license my running clubs so other people pay me to use the name and brand to operate their own small business." "I try to teach them how to keep their running costs low as I know when starting out the costs can skyrocket, so I try to give them the tips of what I did way back in the early days." she said.

Like many budget-conscious business owners, she says she spends little on "the bells and whistles". This means less on broad-based advertising and more on targeted marketing.

John Bishop, director of non-profit organisation PetRescue, uses the same approach. The pet rehoming services, which saves the lives of animals that would ordinarily be euthanized, runs on an extremely tight budget.

"We have the worst business model ever where we don't charge anyone anything," he says.

"We wanted to make it as easy as possible for people looking for a new pet through PetRescue. So one of our primary revenue streams is advertising on our website."

The organisation's funds were boosted when Bishop, PetRescue's only full-time employee, starting taking advantage of Google AdWords to home in on potential pet owners.

"It's probably the most cost-effective form of advertising for us," he says.

Whether you have $50 or $500,000 in the business account is irrelevant; what matters most is knowing your stuff.

The biggest drag on most shoestring businesses is not the lack of knowledge or resources, but the lack of direction and determination. Having passion and clear goals are more valuable than seed funding.

Clarity is not about dollars and cents and it's not about how many clients you have; It's not about your marketing or your cash flow or your balance sheet. All this stuff comes later. It's the heart and soul of why you go into the office every day and the promise you make to your customers.

Our tips for making a budget business run smoothly:

1. Define what is your No.1 goal for the first year in business. Get all the information you need to make a clear and confident decision.

2. Go slow to go fast. Slowing down and putting the right systems in place will mean you later go faster than you could ever have imagined. Being organised makes you go fast. Running around trying to do 100 things at once does not make you go fast.

3. Half of something successful is better than 100 per cent of something that is not. Be prepared to give so that you can have.

4. The five R's - right people, hired for the right roles, who are clear about their responsibilities, getting paid the right money, will deliver the right results.

5. Identify who is your target market. What do they look like? Where do they hang out? What desired outcome are they looking for? When is their highest level of frustration? Why would they choose you? How do you expect them to do business with you?

Chapter 7: Executing Lean Growth Strategies

Lean offers ways to cut work time and eliminate waste whether you are an established or an early stage company. Customer development takes a customer-centric approach to understanding customer needs and problems. The term 'business model' means the design of a business. Business model innovation (BMI) looks at how a business reinvents itself in order gain competitive edge and stimulate company growth. An important part of business design involves being customer-centric.

Many organisations focus on products and solutions versus understanding the problem they are solving for customers. Competition is not just about your products but understanding your customers' needs and your business model.

A friend of mine talks about the big idea, which is really simple; "Get outside your building and talk to customers". This framework is called customer discovery. Talking to customers is nothing new and is a simple concept, but we don't do enough of it to validate and find new opportunities. Too many assumptions are made about customer's needs.

These frameworks have different stages and characteristics including:
1. Understand what is the problem you are solving and for whom.

2. Establish a series of core hypotheses and validate.
3. Determine the product/market fit.
4. Build a minimum viable product (if viable).
5. Feedback, insight and rapid iterations based on data and metrics are key.

In practice, talking to customers is hard. Actions speak louder than words. There is a big difference between what people say they do and what they actually do.

Customers may tell you they are excited about your new product. But in a buying situation their behaviour might be totally different. Customers don't always know what they don't know, so it's through observation that 'insight' is gained.

Henry Ford's famous quote says; "If I had asked people what they wanted, they would have said faster horses". As we know he created the car. Customers will ask for faster horses but we need to apply 'insight' to create new products.

The path for longer-term corporate survival will be in understanding continuous disruption and innovation in the form of new business. Hence embracing methodologies like lean, customer development and business model innovation are important. Why?

While corporates in the past focused on efficiencies, they now need to think about how to reinvent their business models and look for new opportunities. Corporates that cannot manage their existing business models while reinventing themselves will risk disappearing. Over the long term innovating new products and business models is about competitiveness and survival. Examples are:

1. **Xerox:** Introduced the way photocopiers are rented today.
2. **Gillette:** - Makes us buy razors differently.
3. **Ryanair/Southwest/Easyjet:** Allow us to fly cheaply.
4. **Nespresso:** Brings us great coffee (and George Clooney).
5. **Ikea:** Brought us quality design furniture at affordable prices.

These companies have brought new ways of doing business to their industries. They have redefined the way business are done. Companies that don't constantly question themselves how they create value for their customers will have a difficult time to survive over the long term.

Chapter 8: How to Build a Lean and Efficient Business Plan

The concept of the lean startup, looks at how product development cycles can be shortened and businesses can run more efficiently by continuously measuring progress and feedback. This philosophy is particularly relevant when it comes to thinking about your business plan.

In business, it is the continuous planning process that matters. Your business plan, like your business, is a living, evolving, flexible thing. It requires rapid changes and fact-based decision making. I like the body metaphor implied by the term. Lean doesn't just mean thin; it also means healthy, muscular and efficient. Here are five ways to help make your business plan leaner:

1. Make strategy the heart of your plan.

Strategy is focus: Focus on specific target markets using specific products or services. Your strategy is based on some strength or characteristic that links you to your preferred buyers and the solutions you offer them. It defines how you want to set your business apart from the crowd. Strategy isn't text it's concepts. You can summarize strategy in bullet points, using charts or even with a series of images.

To test your strategy statement, read it and ask yourself whether it describes your unique business or could be applied to many others. Is it specific enough to be implemented? Does it define a market, product and branding focus? While everything in a business plan is subject to change, the strategy changes more slowly than the rest of the plan in response to changing conditions.

2. Summarize more, elaborate less.

Your business plan is held up by eight key core concepts: Market, product or services, production, marketing, sales, distribution, management and finance. A fat business plan describes each of these key areas in elaborate detail. Lean business planning means using more bullets and less text. It refers to trends and ongoing assumptions as economically as possible, explaining them in detail only where the detail isn't already understood.

3. Track progress and manage course corrections constantly.

Track your progress with lists and tables full of numbers that you can use to course correct: This is lean to the extent that it's specific, concrete and measurable. The most important part of this is a list of milestones. These are scheduled achievements and activities, each of which ought to have dates, budgets, performance measurements, expectations for spending and sales and specific assignments for task responsibilities.

Aside from these milestones, good planning also needs regularly updated projections of sales, costs, expenses and cash. The projections should be just detailed enough to offer good plan-verses-actual analysis for better management. For example, monthly projections are probably essential for at least the next six months, and usually 12 months is better; but monthly projections beyond a year are most often a waste of time. The goal isn't guessing right (which never happens) but rather laying out the probable results and connecting the dots (like expenses to sales) so you can track progress and make useful changes.

4. Dress up your plan with descriptions.

Descriptions you use to dress up your plan depending on the audience might include market details, technical or scientific background, company history, bios of the management team, generic market research, proof of concept and competitive analysis. Like clothes, you make these descriptions appropriate to the occasion. For example, you might need to prove a market to assure investor or to prove financial stability to assure bankers.

5. Be consistent about updates.

Planning for a startup is a lot like diet and exercise. Business planning is a process, not an event. Like diet and exercise, the key to staying lean is regular repetition over a long time to generate real positive benefits. You don't do it once, or even once in a while. You review and revise your plan regularly.

Chapter 9: Questions to Ask Before Determining Your Target Market

The better you understand your customer, the faster your business will grow. But new ventures often struggle to define their target market and set their sights too broadly. We often overestimate the market size, and in many cases there may not be one at all.

Here are 10 questions that can help you determine whether you have a target market and what it is.

1. Who would pay for my product or service?

First, try to understand the problem that your product or service can solve; then, use that information to help determine who would be willing to pay for a solution. "Not only do your potential customers need to have the problem, but they need to be aware they have the problem. We recommends using Google's keyword tool to see how many people are searching for words related to your business idea.

2. Who has already bought from me?

To refine both your target marketing and your pricing strategy, see who has already bought your product or service. You can gain valuable insights by releasing the product in a test phase and letting potential consumers speak with their wallets.

3. Am I overestimating my reach?

It's easy to assume that most people will need your service or product. But rather than make assumptions, reach out to groups of potential customers to get a more realistic picture of your audience and narrow your marketing efforts. You can conduct surveys, do man-on-the-street type interviews in stores, or organize small focus groups. Sometimes we get so passionate about the idea and how good it is that we overestimate the market size.

4. What does my network think?

As you try to understand your target market, it may be challenging and expensive to seek feedback from potential consumers through surveys, focus groups and other means. But you can tap into your social networks to get free feedback. Many people in your extended network will likely be willing to take the time to give you opinions and advice.

5. Am I making assumptions based on my personal knowledge and experience?

Your own personal experience and knowledge can make you believe that you understand your target market even before you conduct any research. For example, if you are a fitness buff and want to start a business related to personal health, you may assume you know your customer. Don't assume that you can think like your target market. You have to ask them and talk to them to really understand them.

6. What is my revenue model?

Figuring out how you will bring in revenue can help you find your target market. Social ventures can be particularly tricky, because without a specific plan for getting revenue it's easy to overestimate the size of the customer base. But if your revenue model is simply selling a product online, it can be easier to figure out a target customer.

7. How will I sell my product or service?

Your retailing strategy can help determine your target market. Will you have a store, a website or both? Will you be marketing only in your home country or globally? For example, an online-only business may have a younger customer than one with stores. A brick-and-mortar business may narrow your target market to people in the neighbourhood.

8. How did my competitors get started?

Evaluating the competition's marketing strategy can help you define your own target customer, but of course, don't simply copy the marketing approach of your biggest competitors once you define your target consumers. You must have a way of differentiating what you are doing from what the other guys offer.

9. How will I find my customers?

As you start defining your target customers, try to determine whether you can efficiently market to them. You will need to do some market research and study your target audience's demographic, geographic and purchasing patterns. If you are selling from a storefront, you need to know how many people in your target market live nearby. If you are selling from a website, you need to learn about your prospective customers' online behaviour. Understanding how to locate your customers early on can help you establish a game plan once you start building a marketing strategy.

10. Is there room to expand my target market?

Be prepared to redefine your target market or to expand it over time. For example, figuring out whether you are targeting a domestic consumer or customers throughout the world can be a good start. As the power of mobile mapping has grown in the last decade, we have seen the number of target markets grow at our own firm.

Chapter 10: Skills People Need to Create a Lean Business

Lean! Lean! Lean! They are chanting it in corporate boardrooms around the globe. Lean manufacturers, lean business, lean supply chains and lean extended value streams are in various stages of construction by companies looking for competitive advantages in tough markets. Yet, the reality is that only a few companies have achieved any significant measure of leanness.

Why are companies struggling to get lean? Is it lack of top management commitment? I don't think so. CEOs, CFOs, company presidents, and the entire executive staff are all on board. The top guys want all the bottom-line savings and increased flexibility that lean promises. Is it a lack of computer systems that support lean? Not at all. Lean doesn't take a computer. It's a set of tools, or more like a toolbox full of tools and techniques. You select the right technique or method to improve what needs improving. There is no technological marvel to instantly make you lean. Is it the people who work in these would-be lean companies? Now we are getting to the heart of the matter.

Companies are not brands that customers recognize, though a strong brand is important to a company. Companies are not the products that they sell, though the right product offered to the right market at the right price is critical to companies' success.

Companies are not the buildings they are housed in, the web site that represents them in cyberspace, the computers that house their data, or the processes by which things get done. Companies are a collection of people voluntarily banding together to produce a product or service. In order to have a lean business, you have to have lean people and the people have to get lean before the company can get lean. Lean people make a lean business!

What makes lean people? The convergence of three spheres; experience, knowledge, and skill. Specifically, people need experience in the business or industry, knowledge of the tools and techniques of lean thinking, and the soft skills that allow them to put that experience and knowledge to work. While I will touch on experience and knowledge, the main thrust of this chapter is the skills required to take the experience and knowledge and apply them.

Experience

Experience means that, first, you have a thorough working knowledge of the industry in which you work. To have a thorough knowledge of your industry means that you are aware of all the general requirements of the field. You see the big picture that represents your part of the world. Important things you should know about your industry include:
1. Major providers and suppliers.
2. Customers, clients, or patrons.
3. Standard methods of matching providers and customers.

4. Sources of income or funding and how to get these.
5. Specific language used.
6. Specific governing rules or laws.
7. Behavioural norms and expectations and more.

Experience also means you have an extensive understanding of your function in your chosen industry. By your function, I mean the role that you perform within your chosen industry. Your function is your job. Every industry has a set of functions that make it work. A cardiologist has extensive knowledge of how to treat the heart and of how the medical industry works. A house painter has extensive knowledge of paint, painting tools and techniques, and how the home-building industry works. A schoolteacher knows how to work in the education industry, how to teach, and has extensive understanding of the subject she is teaching.

People have sufficient experience to support lean initiatives when they have thorough knowledge of the industry in which they work and the function they perform.

Knowledge

A search of an online bookstore came up with over 17,000 titles on the subject of lean, and that excludes all the books on lean as in dieting. All the books on lean manufacturing or lean business are meant to teach the lean tools and show their application. Clearly, the knowledge part of the puzzle is well covered. Just to make sure we are all on the same page, I will recap the basic tenets of lean thinking.

1. Specify value from the customer's perspective. What is the customer willing to pay for? What makes them choose your product or service over the ones offered by your competition?

2. Map the value streams. Create a clear simple picture of how value is added to your products or services. Understand the physical flow from your suppliers to you and from you to your customers. Include a timeline showing how long things take and all other related detail data. Add the information flows to show where data is created and who gets it when. Link the physical flow with the information flow.

3. Make products flow. Eliminate all stop and store points. Eliminate queues and waiting. Implement takt time cadence.

4. Implement pull systems. Signalling systems align the operations and synchronize all parts of the company.

5. Perfection. Never give up, never surrender; pursue constant and continuous improvement until all non-value added operations are eliminated.

These tenets should be applied throughout the organization, not just on the shop floor. If the goal is lean manufacturing, then you can apply lean thinking just to the shop floor. If the goal is a lean business or a lean supply chain, then lean thinking has to be applied in every division, department, and work group. Lean sales, lean engineering, lean accounts payable, lean customer service even lean plant maintenance departments are required in a lean business.

Lean business are created using tools from that toolbox I mentioned. A short list of some of lean's basic tools includes.
1. Value-stream mapping.
2. 6 sigma quality.
3. The 5 Ss.
4. Visual management.
5. Kaizen events.
6. Cellular manufacturing.
7. Kanban.
8. Single piece flow.
9. Error-proofing.
10. Self-inspection.
11. Line balancing

There is only one problem with these tenets and tools; they have to be applied by people. These are the same people who are doing things the old way today, the same people who have been doing things the old way for a long time, the same people who have a vested interest in doing things the way they have always been done. This is the biggest challenge in getting lean. You have to get the experts at doing things the old way to do things in a new way. Do not underestimate this challenge. Anyone who has tried to implement change in any organization knows that getting the people to change is the biggest problem.

Skills

Back to my main theme in order to have a lean business, you have to have lean people. There are seven skills that make people lean. These are prerequisites to effectively applying lean business tenets and tools. The skills are:
1. Customer consciousness
2. Enterprise thinking
3. Adaptation
4. Taking initiative
5. Innovation
6. Collaboration
7. Influence

Because a company is only as good as its people, these lean people skills are the prerequisites for creating a lean business. Like the tools of lean business, some of these skills are not new in themselves, but they do take on much greater importance for the people of a lean business. We have paid lip service in the past to things like customer responsiveness and teaming. It is time to take them seriously. These lean people Skills should be viewed as a set. Everyone working in a lean business requires them all. A weakness in any skill is the proverbial weak link. It is a flaw that must be corrected. Let's take a look at each of the lean people Skills.

Skill 1. Customer Consciousness

Lean thinking starts with specifying value from the customer's perspective. In order specify value you have to do two things.

a. Know who your customer is.
b. Know what your customer wants and expects.

Everyone in a lean business should be focused on creating customer value. For everyone to be focused on creating customer value, everyone must know who the customer is. This is too often taken for granted. "Of course we know who our customer is," says the CEO of every company; but does everyone, at all levels of the organization know?

If you ask the sales department, they will tell you the customer's name. But what if you ask someone on the shop floor? Does your plant maintenance staff know who your customers are? Try an experiment. Go to your shop floor and ask someone who is building a product who it's for. If you work in a make-to-order industry, they should be able to name the customer. If you are make-to-stock, they should be able to describe the kind of people or kind of company that will use the product. For example, they might say, "This golf club is made for the weekend player of average skill." About another club, they might say, "This is for the professional golfer." The difference between the two in that example may be key to what the customers sees as value.

The idea of internal customers needs to be deepened in a lean business. If your job does not include direct interface with the customer, then maybe you support someone whose job does. To drive the idea of creating customer value through the entire business, we must treat whoever receives the output of our process as our customer. Engineering creates drawings that are used by manufacturing to build the product, so manufacturing is engineering's customer. Sales creates forecasts that are used by planning to buy raw materials and calculate manpower needs, so planning is sales' customer. People should be steeped in that concept and know exactly who their personal customer is.

Knowing your customer is the first step. You then must identify your customer's wants and needs. What do they want? When do they want it? How will they judge if it has value? Find out what the customer wants and needs and measure yourself at meeting those needs. Never get complacent about this. What the customer wanted yesterday might not be what they want today. You need to know what they want as soon as it changes.

Lean people must continually ask the critical customer questions. "Who is my customer?" "What are their needs or concerns?" "Am I meeting these needs?" "How do I know if I am meeting their needs?" Lean people must keep in touch with their customer, identify barriers to customer satisfaction, and eliminate them.

Skill 2. Enterprise Thinking

One of the biggest shifts for a lean business is the shift from functional or departmental thinking to enterprise thinking. Functional thinking causes people to think about their job or their department. When judging the merit of a new way of doing something, they think about the impact on themselves. This causes sub-optimization and territorial infighting. One of the great unseen costs for every business is the cost of defending turf. When a problem occurs, people look for ways to deflect the blame. They spend hours talking, emailing and presenting data about why it's not their fault. When an improvement is suggested they spend even more time trying to make sure the change affects everybody but them.

Enterprise thinking helps people understand how potential improvements affect the business as a whole. Enterprise thinking is where value-stream mapping plays a big part. In value-stream mapping, you map the as-is flow of the entire enterprise. It shows how all the individual activities work together in a process to create value for the customer.

Enterprise thinking can only exist when everyone, from top to bottom, understands what we mean by a process; the conversion of input to output by applying value and when everyone knows that all work is accomplished by a process. The lean business must get to the point that, if something goes wrong, we look at the process that created the waste not the individuals involved. When we want to change something, we look at the steps in the process and change those. Enterprise thinking means we look for the common good not our individual or departmental good.

Enterprise thinking requires that management and the people know the basics of process improvement, which are; process mapping, process measurement, and process redesign.

Lean people are intimately familiar with process mapping. A picture is still worth all those words. Lean people understand various types of process mapping techniques and know when to apply each one. The more tools we have in our process mapping tool kit, the more likely we are to select the proper tool every time.

Process measurement is the key to improving any process. It is still true that most people think, however unintentionally, "Tell me how you are going to measure me, and I will tell you how I am going to act." I have seen the effects of this kind of thinking over and over. A salesman's commission is based on total sales dollars so he pushes the high-dollar items, not the high-margin items. Base the commission on standard margin, and he sells the high-margin items but may reduce actual profit by promising delivery in less than lead-time. The shop then has to work overtime to execute and actual profit is reduced. Measure the wrong thing or measure something in an imprecise way and you may work at improving the wrong area. Lean people understand how to design meaningful measurements of critical steps in their processes.

Enterprise thinking is used to transform the as-is process to the to-be process. The step of reengineering or redesigning processes to eliminate waste requires that lean people set aside their parochial concerns and think about what is best for the entire enterprise. An individual in this position may be asked to modify the process in such a way that it makes his or her job harder but eliminates waste for the larger enterprise. There are specific tools and techniques used to redesign processes. These must be understood and applied by lean people.

Skill 3. Adaptation

Being adaptive is one of the most critical skills for people who work for a lean business. Change technological and social is the hallmark of our time. Change will only accelerate once we start the lean journey. How we react to change today is, in large part, a measure of how we will fare tomorrow. Management must know how to overcome people's resistance to change and how help people adapt their anxiety into productive creativity. Lean people need to know how to adapt the changing environment to their advantage. They both need to know how to recognize reactions to change and channel those reactions into contributions or change them. This is not change management, of which much has been written, but skills for individuals to adapt to a changing world.

When customer demands are constantly shifting, products and processes must change to support each new customer order. Lean people are able to adapt to these changes and execute faster than ever before. Changing processes also means that our roles and responsibilities will change with greater frequency. We may have one job today and be expected to do several different jobs tomorrow. Lean people can adapt to these sudden and frequent changes in their work lives.

There is a continuum of reaction to change from resistance to positive acceptance of the change. We can identify where we or someone else is on that continuum by observing behaviour in a change situation. There are tools that can be used to help people progress through the continuum. Becoming adaptive begins by identifying where a person is on the change acceptance continuum. Then we can select and apply the corresponding tool to move them to the next stage. The lean business must have people who are skilled at being adaptive and at helping others adapt.

Skill 4. Taking Initiative

A lean business can't afford to have people sitting around waiting to be told what to do and how to do it. One of the keys to becoming lean is to identify waste and to take the initiative to eliminate it quickly. In a lean business you don't study the problem, assemble a group of high-level experts to develop recommendations then send the recommendations out for competitive bid. Lean people see the waste in their area of responsibility, talk it over among themselves and take the initiative to fix it now.

Taking the initiative to fix problems means setting goals. Taking the initiative to set your own goals does no good if you can't figure out how to achieve those goals. Lean people have the skills to create plans to achieve their goals. Setting goals and creating plans are great, but lean people must know how to execute their plans. Lean people understand and use basic plan management techniques like setting realistic time-lines and anticipating obstacles so they can be avoided. They know how to execute their plans by prioritizing their daily activities and working on the critical few instead of the trivial many.

One of the biggest wastes in any company is poor personal productivity. Lean people take the initiative to maximize their productivity, manage their time, and stay organized. This old skill set takes on much greater importance given the independence of work in a lean business. Lean people eliminate waste at the personal level as well as the enterprise level.

Skill 5. Innovation

As a lean business empowers its people to eliminate waste as it is identified, to invent new processes and even new products as needs are identified, it will rely on the creativity of its people as never before. It can no longer be the job of just the engineers or staff experts to improve product and process. Improvement becomes the job of every one and lean people will have to be trained to be able to respond.

The lean business knows how to foster and respond to creativity. Lean people know how to analyze problems, apply critical thinking processes, and analysis techniques. They understand the systems engineering approach to the development of solutions so their changes fit into the overall enterprise processes. People need to know how to think in new ways, how to develop creative responses to new demands, and how to be productively creative in applying lean tools.

The first part of developing creative solutions is to understand the issues. Lean people are well versed in the classic analysis tools like Paraeto charts, fishbone diagrams, and control charts. They are also experienced in group brainstorming, and individual creative thinking techniques like mind mapping. Once the issue is understood at the level of facts and data, then we can invent creative solutions. Lean people know about barriers to creative thinking, how to overcome them and the four roles of the creative thinker: explorer, artist, judge, and warrior. Lean people understand different thinking styles and when to apply them.

Skill 6. Collaboration

A lean business has to react fast as opportunities for improvement are identified. There is no longer time to wait to run everything up the management chain or to get new ideas and strategies approved by a large bureaucracy. We have to move now, or the opportunity may be lost. Collaborative groups who know their processes and how they relate to the overall operation allow a company to be much more responsive.

Collaboration between individuals and groups is an important component of any lean strategy. Management in a lean business needs to know how to establish, charter, nurture, reward, and manage collaborative groups. People need to learn what is expected of them in a collaborative environment, how to be team players, the roles and responsibilities of group members and the basic functioning of collaborative groups.

Waving a magic wand and saying you are now a collaborative group does not change ingrained behaviour. Management must determine such things as why create collaborative groups, what are the groups, are they cross-functional or departmental based. Management must decide what authority the groups have. How will the groups be measured and rewarded? What about individual performers within the groups, how will they be recognized?

After management has defined the expectations and limits on the collaborative groups, the group members have to know things like the stages of group development; storming, forming, norming and performing. They must know group roles; leader, scribe, and process observer. An often overlooked tool is consensus decision making. This is a critical skill that collaborative groups have to apply every day.

Skill 7. Influence

The lean business needs to have the entire operation pulling in the same direction to achieve its goals. It needs leaders to make tactical operational decisions every minute of every day that are aligned with the goals of the enterprise. Leaders are not just the people who have formal leadership titles. Leaders are people who influence other people and set the direction that other people follow. Influential people are leaders. Sometimes they influence people in the right direction, sometime not. The lean business needs to identify its formal and informal leaders then get them to use their influence to move the organization in the lean direction.

Influential people should understand what it means to lead, know how to take leadership actions, create and share a coordinated vision, align the organization on what needs to be done, and empower people to get things done.

Welcome to the lean decade. It's a new world; we have to change to keep up. Companies that want to thrive have to align themselves around a set of strategies identified by the term lean business. All the goals of the lean business, reduced waste, faster throughput, reduced costs, and higher profits, can only be achieved through the efforts of its people. To achieve these goals, the people must possess the skills to respond to constant change, constant demand for more, and constant quickening of the pace. The lean business must be sure that its people possess these skills. Acquisition of these skills will not happen by itself. Management must put a plan in place. That plan starts with training, continues with more training, and follows up with even more training. Courses need to be designed or procured. Resources and time need to be allocated. Creating lean people requires management to act. Start right away. The boardroom is demanding it, the competition is doing it, and you can't wait any longer. Lean business are created by lean people.

Chapter 11: Skills of a Lean Leader

Does your company really matter? Would customers suffer a loss if your doors closed?

For most companies, the answer is likely "no,". Recognizing that, companies must set the bar high, providing value to customers in a way that is uniquely their own.

A company we use to work with unique path to astounding its customers has taken the firm on a lean journey. Interestingly, however, their lean journey is not a manufacturing story. When they started their lean journey, it was never about manufacturing. It was about the business.

What are Leaders' Roles in Implementing Lean?

The company's lean journey was about business in that the company was suffering significant cash-flow issues when the new CEO joined the company.

During the new CEO's luncheon speech, he spoke to the audience of his belief that while CEOs must lead a lean initiative, "it is just as important to build leaders at every level to sustain" the effort.

To that end, we will share what he described as seven balance points of lean leadership.

1. Servant leader: Servant leadership is being both a coach and a player. "If you are a CEO, you truly have to know what it is like to walk in the other's shoes. That is servant leadership."

2. Relentless change: "The journey never ends, and we must be learning forever," said the CEO.

He shared several stories to illustrate this point. For example, by 2010 the company had been engaged in lean for many years, with significant "heavy lifting" for more than three years.

"At 2010 we had come a long way since 1999," he said. "We were feeling pretty good about ourselves."

Nevertheless, he also observed behaviours he did not like to see. Having not been at the company during its "heavy lifting" days, new employees did not have the same sense of urgency as more tenured ones, he said. Also, some leaders had strayed from the company's team-oriented approach.

As a result, he changed some of the leadership team in 2010 to better reflect the company's values and keep it engaged in its lean efforts.

He described the moves as "tough lessons" to learn along the lean journey.

3. Disciplined chaos: Disciplined chaos, explains is the ability to recognize where you want to go and remain focused on that goal without letting chaos throw you off.

4. Benevolent dictator: "There is a place where the buck stops, and if it isn't with the CEO, then the business is in trouble."

Further, he says, "there are some dictates."Core values are one example, he says.

The company's core values:
 Be honest.
 Be fair.
 Keep our commitments.
 Respect the individual.
 Encourage intellectual curiosity.

5. Fearless anxiety: See challenges as speed bumps, he says.

6. Cultural revolution: He described a company's core values as its "cement." The revolution is what "goes on above, and the cement allows that to happen."

7. Confident humility: "Confident humility is knowing we will be okay," without getting complacent, he said.

The CEO peppered his talk with a quote from Vince Lombardi and a nod to Jim Collins, author of "Good to Great." He noted that the lean journey can be tough.

"The journey is the destination. When we realize that, that is when we know we have arrived."

Chapter 12: Goals of the CEO in a Lean Organization

One of the most essential aspects of creating a new company is deciding upon the company's overall production and management philosophy. It is the responsibility of the owner, who acts as the head manager or chief executive officer, to guide the company to fulfil its goals. A lean organization is an enterprise that follows a production philosophy of limiting waste to maximize value provided to customers.

A lean enterprise is a company that follows the principles of "lean manufacturing" or "lean production." The goal of lean manufacturing is to get rid of activities that cost money that don't result in value to customers. In essence, lean manufacturing focuses spending as little as possible to produce as much as possible. The CEO and other managers of lean companies should have the goal of implementing and advancing the core principles of lean production.

1. Reducing Waste

One of the goals of lean managers is to reduce waste. Examples of waste-reduction techniques in lean enterprises include reducing the number of non-production workers such as low and mid-level managers, ordering just enough raw material and parts to meet production demands and keeping inventory levels low. When a company produces more than it can sell in short-order or buys more raw materials and parts than it can use in the near future, it has to waste money storing materials, parts and unsold inventory.

2. Continuous Improvement

Continuous improvement is another goal that the managers of lean organizations should work toward. Striving for continuous improvement helps companies improve their production processes and eliminate sources of waste. Allowing employees to provide feedback about production methods and make suggestions for improvement is a way companies can foster continuous improvement and avoid or eliminate safety hazards.

3. Learning from Problems

Another goal that lean managers should work toward is to learning from problems that arise. In businesses that employ a mass-production model, defective products are often cast aside to avoid production stoppages. This avoids costly production stoppages, but it fails to address any underlying problems causing defects. In lean enterprises, production workers stop production when defects arise and work to fix the defect and correct the underlying problems at its root. This can result in more production stoppages in the short-term, but helps eliminate stoppages and waste in the long-term. Managers should also strive to have workers learn the entire production process instead of one narrow role, so that workers can fill in for one another and contribute more when problems arise.

Chapter 13: Lean Strategies for Business Process Improvement

Have you ever asked yourself the Question, "how can I improve my business" or "what business improvement techniques are available to me?" if you have, people generally look at ways to drive sales; however have you ever considered trying to reduce your costs by removing waste to improve your business?

What is waste?

Waste is anything that does not add value for the customer. Traditionally wastes have been grouped together under the following acronym SWIMTOO they are:

1. Scrap/rework: Anything that is a defect or failure, do you ever have to redo something?

2. Waiting: Do you ever find yourself waiting for the process before you to hand you something so that you can begin, or waiting for a phone call, or does your customer have to wait for you to find them their required product?

3. Inventory: Do you have too much of a particular thing or not enough of another, if you work an office do you have a stockpile of items to be worked?

4. Motion: Do you have to move about unnecessarily, if you are making a cup of tea is everything located closely or do you have to travel the kitchen to get everything?

5. Transport: Once you have your product or a piece of your product do you have to move it elsewhere for it to be completed/worked on?

6. Over production: Do you make too many of something, when you photocopy something do you make one extra just in case? Why?

7. Over processing: If a customer expects a certain service do you bend over backwards to give them more? Is that necessary?

There are also others....

8. People: Do you over burden your people or under utilise a certain skill someone has?

9. Communication: Does unclear communication drive unnecessary customer contact?

10. Opportunities lost: Do you do all you can to win or keep customers during your interactions with them?

11. Duplication: Do you or do you make customers duplicate their actions/answers?

Look around your organisation; can you see any of them?

In these lean economic times, business process professionals are watching their budgets get slashed, while at the same time, the hunger for business process management (BPM) and process improvement continues to accelerate across the business.

To meet these conflicting demands, business process leaders should audit BPM projects to eliminate common budget-busters that cause projects to become bloated and unmanageable.

Successful teams have zeroed in on lean strategies that eliminate unnecessary waste typically encountered during process discovery; the first phase of a BPM project that scopes requirements for the process solution. Let's take a look at each of the strategies.

1. Put the right process leaders in charge

To gain a better understanding of process discovery issues, Forrester interviewed 10 leading organizations that have adopted lean strategies that eliminate bloat encountered during process discovery while maintaining the quality of process knowledge and artefacts captured during discovery. We learned that neophyte BPM teams often make the mistake of putting traditional business analysts in charge of process discovery.

These teams quickly realize that traditional business analyst skills for capturing functional requirements are ill-suited to the ad hoc, unstructured nature of process discovery, particularly in a continuous improvement environment. To maintain a lean mindset throughout discovery, leading organizations must put process discovery in the hands of more technical and process-focused business analysts who eat, sleep and breathe business process, embrace evolutionary requirements and bridge the gulf between business and IT.

2. Adopt tools that accelerate process discovery

If you speak with any successful business process executive who has managed large BPM engagements, they will invariably tell you that working side by side in a collaborative and, ideally, co-located environment is critical to success. For example, one BPM executive told us, "We collaborate every day, 12 hours a day."

Yet most BPM suites fail miserably when it comes to providing collaborative work environments that give voice to all of the business perspectives and personalities that contribute to process discovery.

3. Embrace agile approaches

BPM teams consistently fumble when transitioning from the process discovery phase to full-blown development. Process engineers and developers grumble about poorly defined requirements; process owners and stakeholders protest requirements being dropped or not developed to specification.

Ultimately, these back-and-forth skirmishes between process discovery and process development lead to increased project costs and dissatisfied stakeholders potentially risking adoption of the process solution and the larger enterprise BPM initiative.

To create a smooth transition between process discovery and development, successful BPM teams should put process discovery on the clock. Process discovery teams would do well to adopt this same mindset when eliciting requirements for the process solution. Instead of estimating a range of time to complete process discovery say three to four months; successful teams reduce process discovery to the bare bones required to capture the most essential elements of the process solution.

BPM teams should put their process discovery approach under the microscope to detect potential budget-busters and move proactively to tame bloated costs and durations. Focus on using the least amount of time to drive the greatest value, with an eye on continuous improvement.

Chapter 14: Lean Culture Require Enabling Structures

The structure of the organization should be designed for one purpose; to facilitate, and not interrupt, the flow of the core work process.

Culture tends to spin around the core work process of an organization. It may either enable or hinder the work processes that we spend so much time trying to simplify. Lean implementers generally agree that the most difficult part of achieving a truly lean organization is changing the culture.

A Framework for Lean Culture

A good place to start is with a simple framework of what comprises the culture of any organization. Cultures are whole systems, like the human body or the economy. They are complex, interdependent systems and should be redesigned with an understanding of how the different components interact with one another.

Every culture must adapt to the external environment: changes in technology, economy, climate, social trends, resource availability and even the political environment. Having spent a number of years working with production companies, I am well aware how little control they have over the economy, the climate, or political events, which have huge impacts on their business. They can't control them, but they must sense and respond to these changes.

At the heart of any culture are the values, vision or beliefs of the culture. The cultures of the United States, Middle Eastern countries, or any corporation are built on a value system. It is the job of leaders to manage this cultural core and align behaviour and other factors to the core beliefs. Symbols and stories often do the most to pass on and preserve the values of a culture.

The factors that are most controllable and which often inhibit lean implementation are the Structure, Systems, Skills, and Style. If one examines great companies like Toyota, Honda, Intel and others, you will find distinct differences in the key factors of the culture that are essential to their ability to sustain high performance and to adapt to changes in the environment.

Lets take a look at how organization structure may inhibit or enhance improvement efforts.

The Structure of Change Efforts

Change efforts are often structured to their own detriment. Continuous improvement efforts often follow a model that is very similar to the Quality Circle idea (repackaged, of course) of forming teams to address specific problems. These teams use good problem-solving methods, make a recommendation and then dissolve. This can and often does result in useful improvements.

Management is often attracted to this model because it does not require them to make fundamental changes in the way they do their own work or to address the real systems and structure that drive the culture. Lets face it initiating a problem-solving team is easy for management. It sells well.

There is, however, a serious problem with this approach. If a temporary team is formed to find and eliminate waste, one might ask the question, Who created that waste? Did the problem-solving team create the waste? Do they have the power to make truly significant changes? Will they be the ones to follow through on the implementation of solutions, evaluate and learn from those solutions?

Generally, not.

Power resides in the line management teams. Invariably, it was the line management team who made decisions that resulted in the creation of waste. In fact, the management teams own behaviour is often a major source of waste in the organization. Their behaviour and poor decisions are often the root cause. Why, then, are the line management teams not the ones who are analyzing the problem, using good problem-solving tools and making decisions to solve the problems?

The answer is simple. It is much easier for management to appoint a temporary team, with no formal authority, to study and make a recommendation, than it is to look in the mirror and address their own behaviour and solve their own problems.

Consultants are often guilty of being enablers of the problem. It is easier to say to management, Lets form a temporary team, throw some money at it, well take care of it, and you can continue to function as you do, unscathed by the improvement effort.

That may be an exaggeration, but not by much.

If you want to create serious and sustained change in the culture of the organization, you MUST address the functioning of the line management teams. This is the core management structure, this is where power resides. This is where the big money decisions get made.

Structures that Create Teamwork Follow the Flow

I was once asked by a senior executive, Why do we need any structure at all? The question surprised me because it is one of those things we all just take for granted. But, it is a good question to ask.

When you consider what an organization does, it takes in input, processes that input, changes its state in some way, then sells the output to a customer. This is the core work of the organization. Everything, and I mean everything, must add value to this core work. The structure of the organization should be designed for one purpose; to facilitate, and not interrupt, the flow of the core work process.

Second, the structure should be designed to maximize the ability to solve problems and make improvements in the process. Ask yourself whether or not the structure of your organization accomplishes these two objectives. Or, does it inhibit the work flow, creating walls, interruptions in decision making, and separating people who need to solve problems as a unified team?

Most of the organizational structures of our corporations were created in an age in which lean, flow, and rapid improvement was not the basis of organization design. They were not designed to optimize the horizontal flow that serves customers. They were not viewed from the eye of the customer. Rather, they were viewed from the perspective of functional specialization. The focus was on moving up the ladder in the engineering, manufacturing, or marketing department. Up mattered more than sideways teamwork. The customer view is entirely horizontal, and our organization design should first and foremost meet the needs of our customers.

A friend of mine spent considerable time working with a major petroleum exploration and production company to redesign the deep-water exploration and drilling work process and culture, in other words, the whole system. The process is massive. It requires years of work to explore a property, do exploratory drilling, analyze the results, and develop the well for production.

As the design team mapped the process, one thing became clear. There were dozens of handoffs from geologists, to economists, to explorationists, to various engineering departments, etc. Each handoff resulted in redo loops, blame between one group and the other, and delays. But, one thing was missing. No one owned the project and process from beginning to end. It was like a child who was handed off to new parents each couple of years, parents who specialized in the development during those years. By the time the child reaches maturity he would be an orphan for whom no one would take responsibility. Fortunately, we don't raise children that way!

The redesign of this process resulted in one project owner team, who managed the project from womb to tomb. They brought in expert teams as those teams were needed, but they maintained the horizontal view and they were given the necessary authority to make the important decisions that guided the process.

That process now takes less than half of the time it did before the redesign. The primary reason for this success was the creation of organizational structure and decision processes that enabled rather than disrupted the process.

Design from the Bottom Up

When designing the whole system of organizations, I have found it most helpful to design the structure from the bottom up; a zero-base design process. You start with the work process only. You then ask how best to group first-level employees who do the real value adding work. How can you group them around the process to give them maximum control over the process, create maximum learning and improvement?

You design the tools, the training, the information flow, and anything else you can think of to optimize their ability to do their work. These are your work teams.

Once you have done this, you then ask, What help do they need? You don't ask, What is the job of supervisors? You ask the question from the perspective of what will optimize the work of those who create value to customers. Then you form those first-level managers into teams. Again, you ask, What help do they need?

By starting from the bottom and seeking to optimize the ability of each team level, you will find that you often need fewer levels than when you started. You will also create a team structure that follows the flow rather than interrupting the flow. You will create not only a customer-focused process, but also a customer-focused organization design.

Chapter 15: A Lean Business is Customer Centric

A lean organization is committed to its customers and works to minimize waste by focusing all of its resources on producing the best possible value for customers. Investments are carefully considered and only made when it is clear that a long-term financial advantage exists in doing so. Fluff is cut away until all that is left are departments and employees who directly affect the finished product. Any organization can be made lean as long as the organization's mission remains in clear focus.

Conduct an honest assessment of work practices. Change can be tough, particularly when you have been running your business in essentially the same way for years. A lean organization depends upon making the journey from raw goods to finished product as seamless as possible. Look at your current practices in order to determine which can be axed without any inconvenience to the customer. For example, if you purchase raw materials from a distant provider, look to see whether a local manufacturer might provide you with faster service and no shipping costs.

Eliminate the fat. Possibly the most difficult part of streamlining a business is cutting workers. Many companies have found that it is less expensive to outsource their payroll duties, rather than carry a payroll department. Human resource departments can often be run just as efficiently by fewer people as long as the jobs are matched to particular skills. Middle management can sometimes be cut without a corresponding loss in productivity. If you have hired your relatives to work in your business, consider whether they are an asset and how much they add to your bottom line. A lean organization has little room for sentimental hires.

Give employees credit for knowing what they are doing. The reality is that rank-and-file employees often have a better understanding of their jobs than their bosses do. Take advantage of that fact by allowing each employee to contribute in a meaningful way. That could mean encouraging employees to come up with fresh ideas for how to streamline their jobs and to actually implement those ideas. The days of an employer or a manager acting as a "parent" who has all the answers are gone. Businesses simply can't afford to lose the ingenuity that comes with employees who are encouraged to put their stamp on a job. The more weight you allow your employees to willingly carry, the less personnel you will need to see projects through.

Continually revise your method of operation. Becoming a lean organization is a process. Sitting down and devising a plan is an effective way to get started, but you will find that as you look more closely at your business, you will find other areas that need to be trimmed in order to operate efficiently. Look at the process as ongoing as opposed to a one-time fix.

Chapter 16: Profits from the Lean Business Model

When the CEO of the mighty Wal-Mart asks the UK government for protection from competition from Tesco, one fifth its size, it is clear something significant is going on. The rise of Tesco is not explained by its being better at dominating its home trade than Wal-Mart in the markets it serves in the US. Both benefit from enormous scale and purchasing power.

The difference is that Tesco has developed a superior lean business model that is exposing the cracks in the Wal-Mart equivalent. Through its loyalty cards Tesco knows exactly who its customers are and what they want; Wal-Mart does not. Tesco has opened a range of formats to mirror customer circumstances; a strategy which Wal-Mart is just thinking about; and Tesco has developed a rapid, reflexive replenishment supply chain to serve all its formats, including home shopping.

A walk through Tesco's supply chain is an eye-opener. Quite simply, Tesco is getting more of its customers exactly what they want, where and when they want it, and at lower costs. The good news is that none of this is a secret; competitors can follow their example. It is not an exaggeration to call Tesco the Toyota of the grocery business. Tesco is by no means perfect, however and like Toyota, it has not lost the drive to keep improving all of its processes.

Another crack in a very successful business model was also exposed recently. BMW, the proud technology-driven premium carmaker, decided that it could not develop hybrid engines alone (even though Honda is doing so). For years Daimler-Benz and BMW dismissed hybrids as the wave of the future, claiming that diesels and hydrogen were the way forward and that their engineers had all the answers. In the face of the huge expansion of third-generation hybrid car production by Toyota, BMW has joined forces with both Daimler and General Motors to develop hybrids in a bid to catch up. Toyota's strategic path towards developing a new premium position in hybrids is more in tune with present consumer values than a strategy of product proliferation and stuffing cars full of technology that most customers will never want to use.

In every industry the business models of the mass production and mass consumption era are broken or creaking. The 'hub and spoke' airlines which depend on feeding traffic through big hub airports are struggling to compete with 'point-to-point' airlines. Banks and telecoms firms are losing customers as they outsource customer support. Retailers and manufacturers are beginning to question the 'low cost' sourcing of cheap products in China, as responsiveness to customers becomes more critical to successful competition in clothing and footwear.

Maturing computer technology is even undermining the ability of Dell's 'build to order' model; Dell is finding it harder to compete with picking up an equivalent product in the local computer store the same day. The list could go on and on. Add in everyday experiences of waiting in queues for diagnosis and treatment in large general hospitals; or sitting in car dealers waiting to get your car fixed.

Changing times mean that it is time to rethink these broken business models. In each case there are examples of firms that have begun to rethink the latter. These firms are beginning to demonstrate the huge potential of lean management, not only as an approach for streamlining processes, but as a strategy for turning the tables on competitors and providing a better deal for their consumers and employees at the same time. In rethinking the business models, most organisations naturally start by asking what products they should make in the future, what assets they will need to make them, and where the manufacture should be located. Lean thinkers on the other hand begin by asking who the customers are; what problems they are trying to solve in using these products and services; and how best to organize to serve the customer.

It is not the computer, but the combination of the hardware, the software and the knowledge of how to use them that allow us to process documents and send them to others and obtaining, installing, upgrading and replacing all these is a process involving the consumer's time and patience, just like production.

Following this consumption process from end to end reveals that many of the interfaces with the provider's process (which mirrors that of the consumer) are broken and frustrating. Moreover, parts of the process have often been outsourced, so that direct contact with the consumer is lost, and there is no feedback loop to help redesign the product or the processes of obtaining and using it.

In our work on lean solutions, we show how mapping these processes back from the consumer through several layers of distributors to production, and then all the way back to raw materials, reveals really staggering opportunities for removing layers of cost for all parties, including the consumer. It really can be win-win-win for all concerned. In a lean system, better customer service as well as greater convenience turn out to be as free as quality.

The ability to think back from the consumers and to design a provision system that can solve their problems by getting them exactly what they want, where and when they want it, and at minimum cost will be critical to success in the future. The key question will not be who makes the products, but who coordinates the provision of all the elements to the consumer on an ongoing basis.

In the end survival in this challenging environment will depend on the ability and speed with which firms can rethink the business models for their value streams and write off and replace old assets that stand in the way of progress. Firms that are too slow to change will almost certainly be replaced by lean entrepreneurs who figure out how to make lean, consumer-focused business models work. Will you join them or be swept aside?

Chapter 17: Becoming Lean Business with Analytics

It may be one of the lesser known benefits of analytics, but companies can potentially save big money by making use of big data

As I write, scientists are continuing to monitor and analyse data in order to predict the outcome of an eruption at the Bardarbunga volcano in Iceland. It is yet to be revealed whether we will get another ash cloud disrupting European travel as in 2010, but if it is on its way, big data will give us forewarning.

The big data revolution has taken shape. There are now few aspects of business which cannot benefit from the revolutionary trend, and there are few more convincing arguments to leaders, than the opportunity to save costs and drive up profits. Simply through a better knowledge of customers and a greater understanding of business units, any company can significantly lower unnecessary outlay and maximise productivity and efficiency.

There are some very simple means by which larger organisations can reduce costs through data:

1. A better knowledge of customers

To any organisation, understanding customers is essential, however, understanding your customers must go beyond simply knowing the sort of products they like. This needs to be extended to critical facts such as where they live. Knowing that one individual lives with other customers is highly relevant as it is pointless to send out three catalogues to three people who have the same home address, for example. One will suffice, and will also save money.

Equally, an awareness of customer shopping habits or spending will also reduce costs. Some people for example do not tend to buy discounted or reduced items, and others only buy at a discount. It is therefore more efficient in the retail space to market new products to some customers, and advertise that you have a sale on to others. Getting hold of this sort of data, is a relatively simple process for data processing systems and simply allows for focused marketing. There is little point marketing to customers who are not interested. It can be expensive, and will not result in any more or less sales.

One example of a company who saved money by embracing big data is PCM, a large direct marketer of technology products. They found that the money they were spending to acquire customers was actually being used to re-acquire the same customers over and over again.

This is not an efficient use of funds, and a trap that increasing numbers of businesses are falling into. Re-marketing to existing customers is important, but this group do not need convincing that your service is the one for them. This prompted PCM to invest in big data analytics technology that makes it possible to recognise existing customers and to efficiently re-market to this group without having to pay for expensive acquisition campaigns like AdWords.

2. Better knowledge of business units

For many organisations implementing big data projects, the focus has been external, with marketing one of the clearest ways by which companies can benefit from the insight provided. Although this has been the focus, as any CEO will tell you, it is important to gain control of internal costs. A better knowledge of business units and the way they interact and function can allow organisations to maximise productivity, cut waste and therefore save money.

The growth in dependence on IT has provided greater opportunities to monitor the movement of data through an organisation. Data can now hold teams and people accountable. Examining the distribution of data within a company and the results of different business units, leaders can get an overall view of the organisation's direction, identify problematic and over performing units and make changes to maximise productivity and efficiency.

According to a recent report on the Social Economy, investment and acting on social business data can result in a 20-25% increase in knowledge worker productivity in consumer and professional service sectors.

This increase in productivity will result in more creativity, and less time and resources going to waste, ensuring costs are kept to a minimum and organisations get the best out of their staff.

No matter what market a business operates, maintaining agility and keeping costs to a minimum will pay significant dividends. Especially in larger organisations where individual marketing efforts and productivity are more difficult to identify, data can make a real difference in saving money. Saving money is one of the lesser known benefits of big data, and yet another critical reason for businesses to examine the opportunities available within this evolving technology.

Chapter 18: Conclusion

What differentiates a Lean thinking organization from a traditional one? Basically, the Lean thinking organization is grounded in the answers to two simple questions, "What do my customers value?" and "What organization and work processes inside my company will most directly deliver that value?" Answering these two questions through a value-added perspective will help you determine how to structure your work, how to create and share information, and how to measure performance key elements of lean thinking organizational redesign.

The Structure of Work

Lean Thinking demands that an organization look at work differently than the traditional approach. Employees in lean organizations think of themselves as part of a linked chain of operations and decision making points that continuously deliver value to customers whenever the customer request it. In a lean environment people understand how their work relates to the rest of the organization and to the customer. They understand how work is supposed to flow, and how to best utilize their time to minimize or eliminate non-value-added activity (policies, procedures, practices, etc.), so that it does not slow down delivery to the customer.

The lean company makes the flow of work from start to finish visible to all employees. They invest in this understanding with thorough training and cross training. Employees understand how policies and procedures in one part of the organization influence work in other parts.

The all important metric in Lean thinking is time. A lean organization structures work for time reduction. Management concentrates on flowing work continuously. By creating a smoother, uninterrupted flow, they can reduce the cycle time of the entire value stream, thus increasing throughput capacity. Traditional organizations usually manage only the cycle times of their bottleneck operations and neglect the less obvious or hidden operations. These companies allow decisions to pile up between phases and leaving feedback loops that should be customarily closed to remain open. All of this interrupts the flow of work and lengthens customer lead time. As a result, time is wasted and costs increase. Experience across both manufacturing and service industries indicates that less than 5% of the total lead time spent providing a product or service is value-added.

Lean organizations consider where to place responsibility for results and how to co-locate or reposition people and resources to close the white space common in big organizations. They think about balancing the flow of work upstream and downstream, making allowances for how changes in customer demand or product mix will affect this workload balance.

Creating and Sharing Information

Lean thinking companies create more pertinent information and data and share it instinctively. A company seeking to respond quickly to its customers creates fast response among its employees. Work of any kind, whether it's in a financial services company or on the shop floor, is essentially the same in terms of information processing. People process and share information for the purpose of taking actions. Then after seeing the results of those actions, they go through the cycle again. These cycles of learning (creating information, then acting, and acting again) are the heart of an organization, and lean organizations drive hard the sharing of information to shorten these learning cycles.

Lean organizations work like a communication network, with each process performing a particular task and each sending and receiving messages continuously. This communication network is usually manifested in work cells; a group of interconnected employees co-located to quickly cope with the variety and complexity of ever changing customer demand.

Traditional companies, however, instead of allowing the network to speed up information flow, take the opposite approach in trying to cope with variety and complexity. They rely more on adding structure which short circuits the network. If, for example, new technologies are emerging, they reorganize their engineers by technology. If a product is becoming more complex and more and more employees are touching it as it moves through the company, they will increase the number of formal control points and when greater variations in mix of orders show up as they try to increase product variety to the market, they typically build inventories and add slack capacity into the system to handle the overload.

All of this is costly and slows down the company because additional buffers and capacity are not the answers to meeting the demands of the marketplace. In contrast lean thinking companies cope with variety directly by building up their flexibility and greater capacity for creating and sharing information.

Measuring Performance

Lean organizations go back to basics when they decide how they are going to measure and monitor performance. Time, throughput, and team-oriented metrics are the most important performance measures for the lean thinking company. How do lean companies measure time? They follow two rules; keep the measure physical, and measure as close to the customer as possible. Overall measures, such as time from concept to launch of new products or order lead time, are good places to start. Lean organizations measure the cycle times and lead times of all important activities. They start with cycle times of major activities like new product development, or conversion of raw materials to finished product.

Time is more useful as a management tool than cost. Cost is by and large a lagging indicator, a symptom, a set of accounting activities after the fact. Cost is tracked through a set of accounts corresponding to what money is spent on-payroll, inventory holding costs, and so on. Some costs add value to customers, while others are not value-added. Adding cost in the form of better quality raw materials for example, may add value to the customer but many overhead items like rework, inventories, or the cost of other idle assets add cost but no value.

Managing time on the other hand opens up the organization for analysis. Time is an objective measure of current flow, not a calculation based on an accounting chart of accounts. A manager can measure and quantify the flow of activities directly and ask with respect to each whether it is value-added. For example, inventories are idle materials, just as in-boxes contain idle information. Reworking is doing something over. Holding up a decision because of a delay in data arrival is response time lost. As these examples demonstrate, time is a common, direct measure.

Time's major advantage as a management tool is that it forces analysis down to a physical level. Developing a time line of activity of what happened every hour of every day to an order, or to a project, or to whatever you want to monitor tells you exactly what goes on in your company. Once physical activity is revealed, the right questions can be asked: Why are these tasks done sequentially and not in parallel? Why do we do this step twice? Why does this process work only 50 percent of the time? Why do we invest resources to speed this process up and then let its output sit and wait on the next process? Answers to these questions lead managers to where the cost and quality problems of the company actually are.

Of course, all lean companies use both time and cost measures. Cost is the key to knowing financial performance and to controlling the expenditure of resources. But looking at the organization through a physical lens gives management more insight and power in looking for ways to improve results than cost analysis typically can. In most organizations the less time it takes to deliver a product or service the less it should cost.

Lean thinking organizations reduce cost indirectly by squeezing time. When a company attacks time directly the first benefits achieved are usually shorter cycle times, and faster inventory turns. Lower overhead costs usually follow, as the cost of dealing with breakdowns and delays begin to vanish. Lean companies know that if they reduce time they also reduce costs.

The redesign of an organization in harmony with Lean thinking helps it identify value and deliver that value to the customer without interruption whenever the customer requests it. In order to deliver this value Lean thinking organizations must make the flow of work from start to finish visible to all employees by investing in comprehensive training and cross training of their employees. A lean organization structures work to reduce time. Management concentrates on flowing work continuously. By creating a smoother, uninterrupted flow, they can reduce the cycle time of the entire value stream, thus increasing throughput capacity. Lean thinking companies create more pertinent information and data and share it instinctively. They cope with variety directly by building up their flexibility and greater capacity for creating and sharing information.

Time is a very important metric for Lean thinking organizations because they know they can reduce cost indirectly by reducing time. By attacking time directly the first benefits achieved are usually shorter cycle times, and faster inventory turns. This is usually followed by lower overhead costs, as the cost of dealing with breakdowns and delays are minimized or eliminated.

Good Luck!!

www.ingramcontent.com/pod-product-compliance
Lightning Source LLC
Chambersburg PA
CBHW051721170526
45167CB00002B/743